RIDING IN RHYME

A Humorous Poetic Guide to the Equestrian Arts

by
John Anthony Davies

XENOPHON PRESS

Copyright © by John Anthony Davies, 1998
Copyright © by Xenophon Press, 1998, 2021

Illustrations by David C. Bonnett
Cover line drawing by David C. Bonnett
Cover and Interior cover color-rendered by Tracey Arvidson

All rights reserved. No part of the work may be reproduced or transmitted in any form or by any means, electronic or mechanical, including photocopying, or by any information storage or retrieval system, except by written permission from the publisher, Xenophon Press. XenophonPress@gmail.com

ISBN: 978-0933316119

FOREWORD

"Riding in Rhyme" fulfills a desperate need. Most books written about riding, horses and their care are too technical for many too understand but "Riding in Rhyme" can be understood by any age horseman and written as it is in rhyme, also is great fun to read. It definitely is not a book to read and then cast aside to gather dust; it is a book to be treasured and kept close at hand to be read over and over again. Each poem or chapter is a lesson in horsemanship or stable management and the work of a master of both.

"Riding in Rhyme" will be a source of education and enjoyment for horse lovers of all ages.

Lida L. McCowan
Co-Founder/Former President
The North American Riding
for the Handicapped Association (NARHA)

INTRODUCTION

In your hands lies the power

Of the most intelligent, patient
Willing, courageous, powerful

Yet most frustrating dumb animal
On this Earth

Earn his trust, his obedience

His gratitude, and his friendship
Then and only then, can you say

You are a horseman.

This is the challenging postscript to a collection of entertaining and instructional rhymes; a delightful work that will be appreciated by both adults and children.

Mr. Davies, a consummate horseman, has an affinity for children and animals, producing both skilled young riders and well-trained mounts.

This same delightful and soundly academic approach to horsemanship makes this imaginatively illustrated volume unique in its field.

This is a book to be read aloud for the pure joy of its rhymes, while happily learning to become "that true horseman."

Mrs. Arthur T. Anderson
Past President
The United States Pony Clubs, Inc.

LIST OF VERSES

Foreword	i
Introduction	ii
Preface	1
Mounting	3
The Dismount	6
Exercises	7
Forwards Bending	9
Standing in the Stirrups	11
Around the World	13
Now You Know	15
The Seat	16
The Aids	19
The Walk and Halt	20
The Trot	22
The Canter	26
The Rein Back	28
Dressage	31
Show Jumping	32
I Can	35
Grooming	37
Shoeing	38
Diseases and Ailments	41
Feeding	43
Clipping	46
Types and Breeds	48
Lunging	51
Gymkhana Day	52
The Points of the Horse	55
It's a Drag	56
Race Day	61
Cross-Country	64
Combined Driving	67
Today	70
I Saw A Horse	72
In Your Hands	74
About the Author	75

LIST OF ILLUSTRATIONS

Title	Page
Horse and Friend	vi
A Way Must be Found	2
Could Develop a Hump	4
On the Floor Looking Glum	8
Slide in Saddle - Rhythm and Grace	10
Pea Bouncing Round on a Drum	12
A Nip in the Seat	14
Like a Straw-Filled Sack	17
Not Feel in the Midst of a Quarrel	18
He Will Practically Talk	21
Floating and Coasting	24
Thoughts on Growing Old	27
In a Straight Line	30
He Will Sort Himself Out	33
Looping the Loop	36
Diseases and Ailments	40
It Will Massage Away	42
Realize When He Needs a Rest	44
The Tennessee Walker	49
Wrapped in the Rein Like a Mummy	50
The Victors Display their Rosettes	53
Not Trying to Fly	58
In Your Hands / At the End, etc.	74

Illustrator, David C. Bonnet, attended the famous Chigwell Trust Riding Center under the tutelage of the author in the 1960s. He was a prominent architect/consultant, improving access to historical and government buildings for handicapped persons in London, England. He now lives in retirement.

Horse and Friend

PREFACE

Riding and rhyme it could be said
Together form a rhythmic tread

So within these pages it is my intention
To describe the equine and equitation.

Not by the usual methods you'll find
But by planting a rhythm within your mind

For rhythm is needed and never brute force
When you are learning to ride a horse.

So many people have so little time
Or cannot be bothered, so maybe a rhyme

Will help them remember or help them to know
All about horses and what makes them go

And how they regard us, so that in the end
They will know how it feels with a horse as a friend.

"A way must be found ..."

MOUNTING

The first step is obvious, a way must be found
Of getting the rider astride from the ground

But before we can tackle this hazardous task
There is one little question the pupil should ask.

Is everything tightened and tucked into place
For if it is not you may fall on your face

And it's no good complaining or uttering groans
When the saddle should bear all the weight of your bones.

It should never slide under the poor horse's tum
Or you could finish up on the floor looking glum.

So please check the girth make sure it is tight
If the saddle should slip then the horse gets a fright.

When the bridle's put on it should not fall apart
It could give the horse such a terrible start

And the rider would look pretty silly I fear
With nothing in hand to stop or to steer.

So ensure before mounting that keepers are in
Buckles are fastened and cheek pieces trim.

Once everything's tested securely and tried
You may then safely mount from the left or near side

With left hip to shoulder stand facing the rear
The rein on the off side much shorter than near.

"Could develop a hump"

Should you forget this precise simple rule
A nip in your seat makes you feel such a fool.

Now swinging around with a jump and a hop
You stand in the iron looking over the top.

Objectively now it is all very plain
You must get yourself up before lowering again.

In mounting you should not be launched into space
But slide in the saddle with rhythm and grace.

For if you should land with a sickening bump
The long-suffering horse could develop a hump.

Push on your hands while you lift your leg clear
As you swing it out over the so-touchy rear.

Don't polish your boots on the point of the croup
Or you may find you're suddenly looping the loop.

Once you are in contact with saddle and horse
Take up the slack of the reins then of course.

Hands hold the reins, through the bottom they come
Inside the fingers and locked by the thumb.

Now slowly along the fine leather you steal
Until you obtain what is known as "The Feel."

"Feel" is the contact you have with the rear
Without it you will never make it "My Dear!"

THE DISMOUNT

Once you have mounted, you cannot remain
In the saddle too long, you must dismount again

So take your feet out from the stirrups that hang
Swing right leg behind you and don't let it bang.

Drop down on the left till your feet hit the ground
Retaining the reins in your hand as you bound,

Now draw them back over the head after use
Slacken the girth make sure it is loose.

The stirrups cannot be left hanging, it's wrong!
Run them back up to the place they belong.

If they should bang on the elbow, I bet
Bruised joints will result and that means a vet.

Now move to the head and lead the horse on,
Back to the stable from whence he had come

Once you are inside remove all the tack
Brush him all over, especially the back.

When you have finished and rugged him up right,
Close both of the bolts, make sure they are tight.

If you forget and the horse takes a stroll
Out of your bed you may have to unroll

It's not very funny when raining and dark
Searching the fields till the rise of the lark

Only to find when you're chilled to the bone
The horse has decided the best place was home!

EXERCISES

Physical jerks play a major part
In teaching the rider the noble art.

In no other sport is there so much demand
On the muscles and joints we have to command.

To learn to coordinate thought into deed
The mind of the rider must be highly keyed.

If the mind is asleep then the body will wallow
So we must decide the best action to follow.

Let us ensure that the brain is alert
That the body is supple then we may avert

The risk of confusion or perhaps getting tired
For a strong will and body must be acquired.

On the floor looking glum

FORWARDS BENDING

When bending forwards on the pony's neck
You don't have to look like a physical wreck.

As long as you listen to what you are told
Place both hands on hips relinquish your hold.

The reins are not wanted when you're going down
If you hang on to the mouth the instructor will frown.

Bend from the waist and grip with the knees
Keep lower leg where it belongs if you please.

Hold your head high with back nicely hollowed
Hair doesn't taste very nice if it's swallowed.

Don't bury your face in the crest of the mane
Look twixt the ears till you come back the same.

If you let your head drop while doing this chore
You'll have to dismount for your hat on the floor.

The good that it does you is all very plain
You'll find you can do it again and again.

"Slide in the saddle with rhythm and grace..."

STANDING IN THE STIRRUPS

To stand in the stirrups takes balance and nerve
But provided this method is strictly observed

And you closely adhere to the rules that I mention
You will soon obtain balance without any tension.

To lift from the saddle with great "Savoir Faire"
Push as if rising up out of a chair

By straightening the leg as the knee grips the roll
Press down and lift up from the iron on the sole.

Now pulling your seat in and keeping head high
Prevent loss of balance by closing the thigh

Should lower leg swing out of line you will find
The horse has moved on while you're left behind.

So pull in your seat and hold your position
By balance alone without slightest suspicion

Of using the reins or the front of the saddle
Reins are for hands to control not straddle.

When up in the air you maintain your height
By making the knee and the thigh close tight

When you are ready return to the seat
But slowly remember to finish off neat.

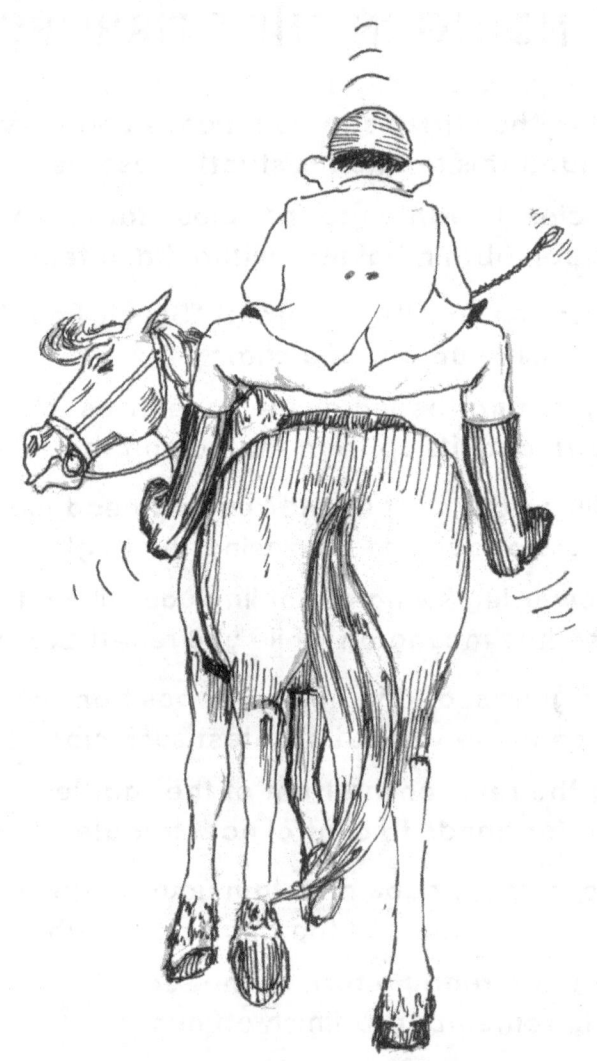
"Like a pea bouncing round on a drum"

AROUND THE WORLD

"Around the World" is more like a game
But it takes some doing just the same
When introduced as a light-hearted race,
The competitive spirit will fall into place.

Children especially derive heaps of fun
Without realizing the work they have done
It demands a great deal from a physical stance
As well as improving their sense of balance.

Take care that you not attempt it too soon
Or some nervous pupils are liable to swoon
The game as its name would likely suggest
Keeps riders revolving around till they rest.

Finally back whence they came safe and sound
With never a hand or a leg on the ground
That's the intention although I must say
Sometimes the students get carried away.

They throw up their hands and with legs all at random
They spin themselves earthwards with gayest abandon.
Starting with legs on one side of the horse
They really don't stipulate which side of course.

Lift them well up and clear of the ears
Until facing sideways your body appears
Now other leg lifts and once more you turn
So now you end up looking over the "stern."

In this unsafe position you cannot remain
So continue to pivot till facing the mane
Once you have circled, twisted or twirled
You can surely announce that you've been 'Round the World!

"A nip in the seat"

NOW YOU KNOW

The physical jerks that I have described
Are but a few that can be contrived.
There are for many more that a rider can do
That will strengthen him physically, mentally too.

There's clapping the heels in front and behind
Toe and leg lifting, both are designed
To strengthen the joints and develop a grip
Then there's trunk twisting which supples the hip.

If arms and hands circling should worry or thwart us
We may take a rest lying back on the quarters.
Once body is supple and strengthened enough
The teacher can now really start getting tough.

By putting the rider through various paces
Both pupil and horse can begin going places.
Then hopefully one day a ribbon of blue
Will make all this hard work so worthwhile for you.

THE SEAT

Oh dear, what a calamity
The seat is the prime part of your anatomy,
Use it, abuse it, in all riding strategy
Without it, you've had it I fear!

As you shall walk, so you will ride
No matter how hard you try to hide
The fact that you slouch or hump the back,
Will still make you look like a straw-filled sack

You must endeavor to sit at ease
With your weight in the center of spine and knees
Up from the iron which lays back from the toe
The heel should press down, no daylight must show

Between knees and the roll on the forward flap,
While the thighs grip the saddle and loose stirrup strap,
If you are a rider with thighs rather fat
Then riding has even a cure for that!

It will massage away but that will come later
For now lets consider a subject much greater.
The hands make the rider, believe me it's true
With bad hands the horse cannot know what to do.

So if you will humor me for a while
I will try to describe the true riding style.
Hands stay apart, five inches enough
Not clasping as if they are tucked in a muff.

Should you clamp fingers as if you are knitting
The bit in his mouth could send him off spitting
And don't rest them down on the withers or pommel
You will not get feel in the midst of a quarrel

"Like a straw-filled sack"

The reins should be equal for him to react
To the rider's commands through elastic contact.
The elbows stay naturally close to the hips
While a straight line runs down through reins to lips

The body should stay quite erect but relaxed
While the head is held up not forward collapsed.
To finish the line we must correspond
The heel, thigh and shoulder, which will form a bond

Between rider and horse on a vertical plane
Then aids can be given without undue strain.
When you have acquired this position so neat,
You can truthfully say you've developed "The Seat."

"You will not get feel in the midst of a quarrel"

THE AIDS

The aids are the way we transmit our intentions
Without undue fuss or severe complications
Concentrate mainly on seat, legs and hands
The voice is another the horse understands.

There are other "aids" that can also be used
But care must be taken they are not abused
Whips, spurs and martingales these are but three
That can help you provided they're used sensibly.

They should merely assist in the schooling or training
Not punish the horse even when disobeying
So let us forget these inventions so neat
That will never completely replace legs or seat.

Of the aids we possess the seat is important
For obtaining collection, a name for deportment
Together with legs it draws on the drive
From behind, which is how the impulsion's derived.

The hands then take over, together with back
Drive the horse forward on one single track
The voice is found useful to scold or to settle
A horse that is likely to be on his mettle.

But care must be taken to ensure that all three
Work smoothly together and not contrary
For nothing will worry or upset the horse more
Than a rider who dithers or isn't quite sure.

Now I've explained what the aids really are
You can start to apply them perhaps you'll go far
The day will soon come he will practically talk
Before that day dawns you must first learn to walk.

THE WALK AND HALT

The horse should walk on with a firm four-beat rhythm
The rider, of course, must ensure he moves with him.
Anticipate movement with strong back and seat
Endeavor to maintain a firm steady beat.

To keep the horse moving and in a straight line
Will take all of your patience and most of your time.
But nevertheless you must try to sit
Deep down in the saddle, drive up to the bit

With both legs in unison close on the girth
Drive inwards and forwards for all you are worth.
As the horse then responds and moves into his stride
Take up the feel of the reins on each side.

Now you can try things like circles and turns
Remember to praise him each time as he learns.
Be patient yet firm, he will give of his best
Provided you realize when he needs a rest.

Once you are ready collect him again
But in between work let him have a long rein.
When he can walk on he must learn how to halt
Without undue strain or a sudden sharp jolt.

So let the horse know that it is your intention
By shortening the reins without apprehension
Drive up to the bit and restrain with your hands
This is the language the horse understands.

As he slows down apply both legs at will
Until he's collected and perfectly still.
The horse should halt firmly four feet on the ground
Without any twisting or turning around.

Once he can do it without getting hot
We can then safely say that he's ready to trot!

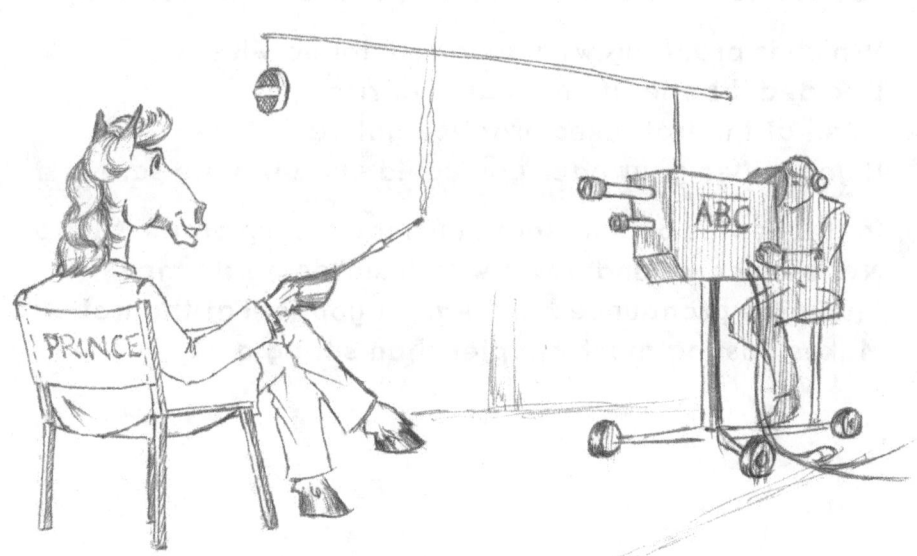

"He will practically talk"

THE TROT

When the horse can walk on with impulsion when asked
You may then attempt a more difficult task
The trot is a pace that will make you or break you
Provided your nerve doesn't go and forsake you.

The new rhythmic pace moves from four into two
Which right now may not mean a great deal to you
But when you are trying to sit at the run
You can feel like a pea bouncing round on a drum.

Which is probably why an instructor so wise
Decided it better if one learnt to rise
To sit at the trot takes practice galore
If you stiffen your back you could end up quite sore.

In the depths of your seat you should cushion the bump
Not bounce up and down with a sickening thump
The more pronounced movement you feel at the trot
Makes posting much simpler than sitting a lot.

Rise out of the saddle, push up from the knees
Angle the body 'bout forty degrees
Don't lift the seat up in the air too high
You are learning to trot, not trying to fly.

Keep your hands low don't gesticulate
Like tossing a pancake up out of a plate
To drive the horse forwards the aids are the same
As the walk, but you merely repeat them again.

Keep driving with seat to maintain the impulsion
Don't lift too soon or rise in slow motion
When you are ready to make the transition
Collect your horse in and secure your position.

Driving downwards and forwards with legs at his side
Apply the aids firmly, move into the stride.
When you start rising remember take care
Observe when you're on the diagonal pair.

"Floating and Coasting"

You lift as the leading leg forward flows
Returning once more as the opposite goes
If you should rise on an incorrect leg
You will feel like a man with a stout wooden peg.

Don't stay one-sided, your balance will suffer
Change leg with your horse then you will discover
You've mastered the trot both sitting and posting
And will literally find yourself floating and coasting

Through circles and turns and figures of eight
That will lead to the canter, at some future date
But whether you learn how to canter or not
At least you can say that you've mastered the trot.

THE CANTER

To canter smoothly on a horse is easier said than done
He must remain collected and should never try to run
If he takes the bit between his teeth when in the trot
He will never ever canter but will gallop like as not.

Nothing's more frustrating than a horse that's taken hold
Particularly when the rider has some thoughts of growing old
But if you have progressed this far without becoming parted
Remember this, take heart my friend, your troubles have
    just started.

The cadence changes once again from two now into three
With a period of suspension, although some may not agree
But if you try to find this out before your seat is sound
Then you may be suspended just before you hit the ground.

So leave the technicalities and get on with the task
Of making the transition precisely when you ask
Before you give the aids again remember the old rule
Of sitting and restraining in a corner of the school.

For on a bend a horse should flex in the required direction
Which makes it easier to obtain his balance and collection
Keep inside leg closed on the girth, assist the horse to bend
A guiding hand maintains the feel, your seat its weight
    should lend.

The outside rein should now support the contact all the while
Until the aid is given to strike off in flowing style
Then once the horse is moving at a steady rhythmic pace
Maintain impulsion from behind, restrain the urge to race.

The canter has of all the gaits by far the smoothest stride
Which may be just as well when jumping fences high and wide
So let's move on and try our hand negotiating courses
That are designed to test the skill of riders and their horses.

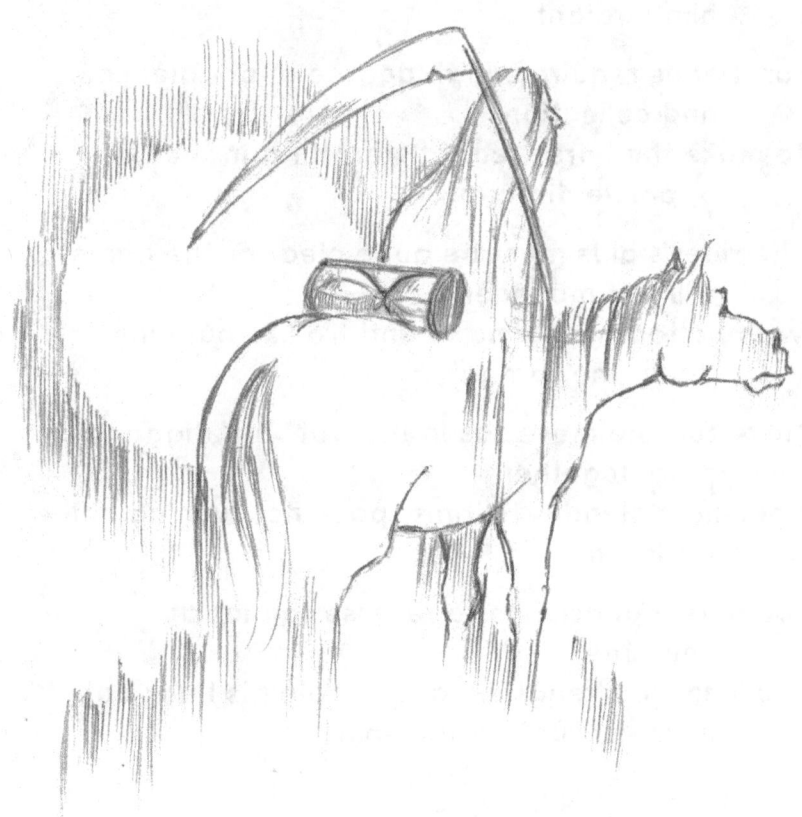

"Thoughts of growing old"

THE REIN BACK

The rein back to a horse they say is not a
    natural gait
Some riders find it difficult to reverse yet keep
    him straight

For it does require a high degree of obedience
    and collection
To make the horse retreat stern first in the
    opposite direction.

The rider's aids must be quite clear or the horse
    will just meander
With bottom waggling to and fro like humans
    doing the samba

Make sure he moves as in the trot with diagonal
    pairs together
Keeping a steady rhythmic pace not rushing hell
    for leather.

You must not ask him to reverse too far at
    any time
You want to strengthen and supple his back not
    injure or rupture the spine.

So ask of him gently, don't fidget or fuss, or jerk on
    his mouth with your hands
Use both legs and seat to close him right up till
    ready collected he stands.

Ease him back quietly your legs by his sides
    maintaining the feel al the while
Until he moves back for a number of strides
    without ending up in a pile.

This movement done smoothly will help a great
    deal when finally you do venture out
Into the land of the fox and the deer to the sound
    of the Tally-Ho shout.

But you may feel quite silly if you do have to halt
    when out hunting and then have to wait
While a spotty-faced kid on her well-schooled
    horse reins back and opens the gate!

"In a straight line"

DRESSAGE

Dressage is a dirty word to hunters,
It sometimes makes them tremble quite a bit,
And mention of the word to a show jumper,
Will often make them throw a tantrum fit.

It surely is not fair they say to ask them
They're trained to chase the fox and follow hounds,
And jumpers "fly the fences" for the askin',
The dressage ring is really out of bounds.

So many are the things one must remember,
Like stepping sideways while remaining straight,
Or movements known as Travers or the Renvers,
Moves forwards early or reverses late.

Now if you think this whole thing is confusing
Just try the Piaffe or Passage on for size,
And if you're in the mood to do some musing,
You could end up a deal more worldly wise.

For dressage is a word that means precision,
Most certainly it's difficult to do,
With repeat, repeat, repeat and then revision,
You really get to know each part of you.

But secretly the riders will admit it,
There is something to this dressage thing you know.
If only you can really try and stick it,
The agony is worth it all somehow.

For when you ask the horse to pay attention
As you approach that horrifying ditch
Perhaps you will agree and maybe mention
That dressage really has its little niche!

SHOW JUMPING

To complete a varying course of jumps
Without any faults and very few bumps
Takes courage, skill and luck as well
To finish together at the final bell.

You must learn how to judge the approach with your eye
Not hang on and wait with your hopes in the sky
In no other sport is there so much demand
On the senses the rider has to command.

The horse and rider must be as one
Though the ground work perhaps isn't so much fun
It's the work on the flat that produces results
Without it you only produce stops and bolts.

So give your horse time don't hurry too fast
Remember the saying about he who laughs last?
When the final day comes you attend your first show
Without any doubts and ready to go.

Don't wait in the ring at a stationary stance
Keep your horse moving give him a chance
There goes the bell it's time to depart
Into a canter and up through the start.

Head straight for the first fence do not let him race
Hold him right, back to a collected pace
Now here comes the jump its a brush and rail
Look for the next one as over you sail.

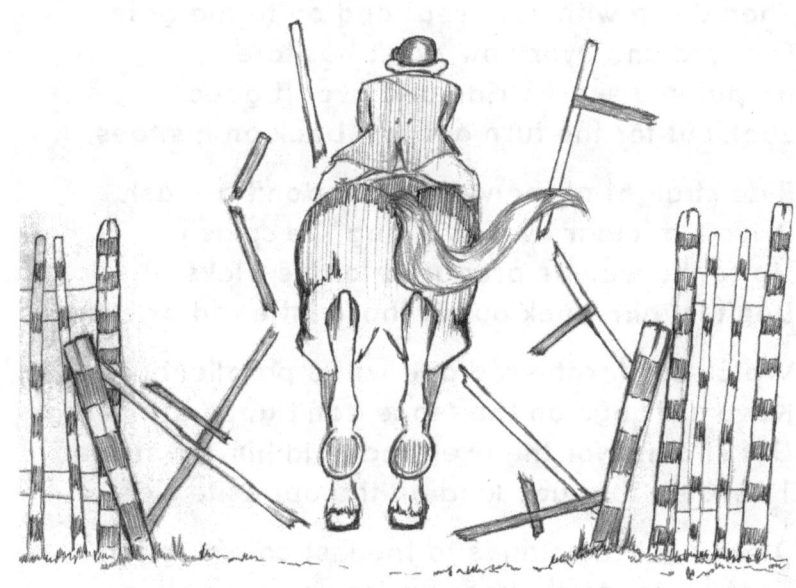

"He will sort himself out"

It may be a spread over six feet wide
So gather him into a balanced stride
Now urge the horse on and follow him through
With your hands till you're over number two.

Then down with your seat and on to the gate
Forward and over now don't hesitate
He put in a short stride and over it goes
Look out for the turn get him back on his toes.

Ride straight at the water now don't go rash
Drive him clear over avoiding the splash
Up to the wall be prepared for his tricks
Don't let him duck out of those little red bricks.

Watch out for the red and white parallel bars
Keep your eye on the fence don't gaze at the stars
Get straight for the oxer and hold him on stride
To ensure that you land on the opposite side.

Down past the stands to the last combination
That someone thought up for your ruination
The first and one stride, the second and two
Relax now at last you are finally through.

Only four faults but you could have gone clear
If you hadn't decided to interfere
Always remember that if you're in doubt
Leave the fellow alone he will sort himself out!

I CAN

I cannot walk or run or play
A game of tennis every day
I cannot dance or ride a bike
I'll never know what skating is like

I have no soccer boots or ball
They are no use to me at all
I'll never ski the waves or snow
So many thrills I'll never know.

I'll never sail the wind or surf
Or chase a ball across the turf
Nor climb the snowcapped peaks above
So many things I'll never love

But I can ride through forest trails
View the fox and rabbit's tails
Watch the geese and ducks in flight
While leaping stags and deer take fright.

I can follow mountain tracks
Past climbers weighted down with packs
To trace a river to its source
Above the clouds and feel the force.

Yes, I enjoy the Sport of Kings
When carried high my feet take wings
To fly me on a pleasure course
For I Can mount and ride a horse...

Dedicated to the Canadian Therapeutic Riding Association (CANTRA)

"Looping the loop"

GROOMING

Now let us think about grooming the pony
Brushing each day is not all baloney
To help him stay healthy then grooming's a must
It removes the loose hair and gets rid of the dust.

It relaxes the muscles and tones up the blood
So the pony keeps fit and never goes dud
Start with the curry comb, rubber of course
The metal's for brushes and not for the horse.

Now on with the dandy for cleaning off grime
The body brush next for making him shine
Water brush oughta crush sticking up manes
And lay down the tail if you're taking great pains.

Take up the hoof pick to clean out the feet
Then damp sponge and duster to finish off neat
The mane can be braided with needle and thread
Odd up the crest and one for the head.

To groom a horse properly will take you some time
To leave him uncared for is surely a crime
For it is so rewarding to hear the judge say
"That's the best cared-for pony I've seen here today!"

SHOEING

Horses' feet need particular attention
So maybe it's as well to mention
A few of the things that a farrier can do
To ensure that your horse will always go true.

To be certain the feet will stay healthy and strong
Shoes must be checked as a month rolls along
They may be left on for six weeks or more
But then there's a risk of the feet getting sore.

When horses are shod be it hot iron or cold
There are points we should note that will help them to hold
The clip that is made to fit at the toe
Should be broad and even and arrowed in low.

Nails that secure must be driven in tight
Between the edge of the hoof and the line that is white
When they appear through the wall at the side
The clenches are turned down and hammered out wide.

Heels should be level and well opened out
There cannot be any sharp edges about
The shoe must rest level no daylight at all
From the flat of the iron to the edge of the wall.

The sole and the frog may be trimmed but with care
Or the elasticity of the heels will not wear
A farrier can help to improve conformation
By fitting a shoe that corrects faulty action.

You may think it's easy to make a new shoe
But blacksmiths can make their own tools too!
There's a thing called a buffer, one called a stamp
A parer or searcher, a tripod or ramp.

There are foot or hoof nippers and a sharp pritchelin
That enlarges the hole when the point is knocked in
A weighty iron anvil with a large beaky horn
A razor sharp knife that exposes the corn.

Then tongs are for holding the shoe when it's hot
If you count all his tools you will find quite a lot
The blacksmith will make and shape each one of those
Which is probably why you must pay through the nose.

But it's worth every penny for your horse to stay sound
Particularly when working on rough or hard ground
If you skimp on your shoes you'll save money of course
But please do remember, no foot means no horse!

"Diseases and ailments"

DISEASES AND AILMENTS

Man's oldest friend can frequently suffer
Like humans from ills they catch from each other
They itch and they scratch and get terribly sore
To treat them can really become quite a chore.

Things like the sweetitch and ringworm and mange
Cracked heels and sore backs and then for a change
You may find a horse with thrush or a quittor
Or a mare that's in foal, which could mean a bed-sitter.

Sickle hocks and capped hocks tendons that twist
Warbles and stomach bots and large serous cysts
Pricks from a nail or worse a bruised sole
A fistulous wither a large gaping hole.

Then ponies like children, are prone to the colic
Particularly if drinking when hot from a frolic
Splints twixt the tendons and thoroughpins behind
Worms there are plenty of various kinds.

Horses forge and speedy cut, overreach as well
They trip and they stumble, just why we can't tell
They suffer from many outlandish diseases
Like the cough and the strangles and long-winded sneezes.

Sand cracks, split hooves and severe laminitis
Spavins and ringbone, prolonged lymphangitis
They whistle and roar, get false quarters and all
Til one often wonders how they stand so tall.

Be that as it may, they somehow survive
All the devious hardships we humans contrive
But just working with them through trouble and strife
Can help us to get so much pleasure from life.

"It will massage away"

FEEDING

Horses in their natural state
    Will eat continuously
They wander as from plate to plate
    Just grazing so you see.

When humans stable them inside
    They change the plan somehow
So follow "Mother Nature's" guide
    Feed little and often now.

The horse's stomach is quite small
    It lies against the lungs
Exerting when it's very full
    Could pop out all their tongues.

So let them drink before they eat
    Not wash down all that grain
Or that could really cause hot feet
    And colic's such a pain.

You'd better feed according to
    Their ages, work and size
For if you regularly do
    They'll bloom before your eyes.

Don't scare them with a sudden change
    In diet or time of day
Cheap musty oats can cause dry mange
    While coughs come from bad hay.

The food they eat is very plain
    So it would seem to us
That when they really get good grain
    It could cause quite a fuss.

"Realize when he needs a rest"

Good oats are golden plump and clean
      They can be bruised or boiled
Barley can be cooked in steam
      Providing it's not spoiled.

Then horses love their little treats
      Like carrots, corn and maize
Molasses cubes and other sweets
      Should not become a craze.

A staple diet is what they need
      Especially good hay
So just be careful what you feed
      Then you will "make their day."

It takes too long to put back on
      What they have taken off
You can't undo what has been done
      Though you may surely scoff.

When work begins digestion slows
      So after you have fed
Allow the horse to stand and doze
      Or wallow in his bed.

Treat them right and keep them tight
      Recall the adage, that
A hungry horse is mean of course
      But the groom's eye makes them fat!

CLIPPING

"To clip or not to clip, that is the question.
Whether to clip early or late in the fall
Or whether to clip at all."

It certainly seems very queer
To take off at this time of year
When the cold winter winds start to blow
And the temperature drops way below.

But nature will take care of that
By providing a warm layer of fat
That will keep the horse cozy and warm
Through the coldest of all winter storms.

Though nature they say does provide
What horsemen must really decide
Is what type of clip they should make
And just how much hair they should take.

We just cannot leave them all bare
That would make all their horsey friends stare
And horses have feelings you know
So we really should watch how we go.

The clippers won't penetrate stain
So maybe I'd better explain
A few little tricks of the art
That will help you before you can start.

The coat should be thoroughly clean
So that ridges or lines won't be seen
And the blades must be frequently oiled
Or the stroke that we make may be spoiled.

So don't set the clippers too tight
For the horse gets a terrible fright
If they catch in the coat or under the throat
And we really don't want him to fight.

So don't push the blades in too deep
Let them glide with a long even sweep
And brush the loose hair as you go
Or you'll find they get awfully slow.

And the horse cannot stand there all day
While you dither and "nitpick" away
For the blades will become rather hot
Which the horse doesn't care for a lot.

You know it's a wonderful thing
What nature will do in the spring
When the coat grows again bright and new
But remember it's all up to you!

TYPES AND BREEDS

Horses and ponies come in all shades and sizes
Among them you'll find there are many surprises
Brown ones and black ones, both are called bays
White ones and dapple ones, these are called grays.

Red coats and blue coats that horsemen call roans
Chestnuts and Duns the color of stones
Skewbalds and Piebalds, mistaken for cows
Liver and strawberry should you wish to browse.

We seldom find reference to black or white
It seems only the Arab horse has this right
He we are told, is a class on his own
The King of the Equines, unchallenged his throne.

The Thoroughbred also is high up the tree
Arab blood runs in his family
A white horse remains though it's called the Albino
But do not confuse with the cream Palomino.

There's the American Quarter and Saddle Horse too
The Pinto and Mustang (or Bronco to you)
The gay Appaloosa that's freckled all over
The Tennessee Walker's a bit of a rover.

All over the world there are breeds aplenty
But never so varied as England's fair country
They have Clydesdales and Cobs, Dartmoor and Dales
Exmoor and Fell that breed in the vales.

Hacks bred for ladies and Hackneys that trot
Hunters for gentlemen who still like them hot
New Forest and Welsh are the ponies kids ride
While the Shetland and Shires take it all in their stride.

Then there's the Suffolk seen pulling the plow
It's a pity we don't see him very much now
But then that is progress, so some people say
But I'd sooner drive horses than cars any day...

"The Tennessee Walker"

"Wrapped in the rein like a mummy"

LUNGING

When backing, breaking, bitting or making
    A horse can be put on a rein
Sent round in a circle at the walk, trot or canter
    Without any undue strain.

Do not stand still for you're sure to get dizzy
    Or wrapped in the rein like a mummy
While the horse rushes round like a dog in a tizzy
    Or a bull with a bee on his tummy.

Keep the rein taut and retain a few loops in your hand
    So you can let it out
Should the horse throw a fit or take up a stand
    To fight you or mess you about.

Don't stop the fellow from having his fun
    He must get it all out of his system
Before he can settle and get the job done
    And respond to your few words of wisdom.

Remember each session must not be too long
    Or the horse will get terribly bored
Little and often will do him more good
    Don't continue until he is floored.

Move with the horse and vary the paces
    Changing the rein now and then
So you can prevent him from pulling those faces
    The next time you lunge him again

The horse should enjoy his brief spells with the master
    Not look upon them with distaste
But if they repeatedly end in disaster,
    Then all that you've done is a waste!

GYMKHANA DAY

All over the country from May to September
From farmhouse and city the youngsters remember
The day they have worked for the whole winter long
Schooling their ponies and making them strong.

Just to compete in a local horse show
They rise with the lark and make ready to go
Tack is all polished, ponies all bloom
They seldom receive such a vigorous groom.

On goes the tail guard to stop rubbing sore
Then knee pads and bandage till ready for war
Into the horse van up from the back
These are the lucky ones, others must hack.

When they arrive off with the blanket and rug
Enter the fray like a bull-nosed old tug
Mount now and line up amidst all of the din
Who cares about manners the first home will win.

"The victors display their rosettes"

The battle is fierce for the prize to be won
And many a rider will fall in the sun
When racing the horse at faster paces
Without risk of him kicking over the traces

The flag race, a sack race and obstacles new
Bareback and bending round poles weaving through.
Walk, trot and canter or else saddling up
Ribbon and needle, the ring and the cup

Musical sacks or the trot and the lead
The potato which horses consider as feed.
Run, mount and gallop. Ride down in pairs
Chase somebody's Charlie that rises like stairs.

When it's all over the journey back home
The skewbald and piebald, chestnut and roan.
"The victors displaying their rosettes so gay"
That flutter from bridles on Gymkhana Day.

THE POINTS OF THE HORSE

There's the Forelock and Forearm,
   the Croup and the Dock
A Chestnut and Ergot,
   the Knee and the Hock

Or else there's the Fetlock,
   the Pastern and Sole
Shannon or Cannon Bone,
   Stifle and Poll.

The Point of the Shoulder,
   the Point of the Hip
The Angle of Heel,
   or the Curb of the Lip.

The Frog and the Wall,
   or the Loins near the Flanks
The Withers and Ribs,
   number eighteen in ranks.

The Back and the Quarters
   that carry our weight
While Tendons and Ligaments
   ensure he moves straight.

The Coronet and Crest,
   or the Heel and the Toe
To remember them all,
   you surely must know

That these with the Muscles,
   and most of the Joints
Together are known as
   the "Horse's Good Points."

IT'S A DRAG!

The day of the hunt dawns
    a crisp autumn morn
When horses and hounds
    meet again on the lawn

The horses excitedly
    champing the bit
The hounds scratching holes
    where they dither and flit

With sods flying high
    in the sweat-steaming air
But nobody heeds them
    nor yet seems to care

Riders and followers
    exchanging the chat
About breakfasts and
    stirrup cups, this and that

"Did you hear what that puppy
    received for a name?
No one will think up
    that letter again!"

You can hear the whips
    calling out loudly and clear
"You mangy old cur,
    get your hide over here!"

The sound of the horn
    brings the whole scene to life
As the master sets off
    with somebody's wife

The whole field will follow
        with colours in front
The others behind
        in the rear of the hunt.

Tradition is held
        to the bitter extreme
If you fall on your head
        you never dare scream

Bad manners are frowned on
        it's not really nice
To swear or blame horses
        that put you down twice

It's the day for good sport
        when most everyone
Takes ditches and logs
        at a galloping run

"Make way for the staff,
        move your horse over there!"
"A beautiful day Marm
        I do declare!"

"Hold Hard! Hold Hard!"
        There comes the cry
"Horses weren't meant
        to damn well fly!"

"Not trying to fly"

There's always the little chap
    way in the back
Who rides "hell for leather"
    but came for the hack

The drag way out front
    is the scent they all chase
Through mud and high water
    at a hell of a pace

Through long grass in meadows
    and close knitted trees
That whip up the hind legs
    and bruise knotted knees

"Hold Hard! Hold Hard!"
    the mournful sound
Somebody's fallen there
    down on the ground

"Make way for the Doctor!"
    "Oh they'll be okay.
They'll all live to hunt
    on another fine day."

It's part of the hell of it,
    part of the fun
The risk, the excitement,
    the day to be won

And when it's all over
>	the journey back home
The grey and the chestnut,
>	the bay and the roan.

The stories where everyone
>	changes the names
About the randy old stud
>	and the horse with no reins

Who jumped o'er the coop
>	with a hound on the top
The rider admitted,
>	he just couldn't stop!

The tales will be retold
>	but never the same
About the day they went live
>	and the brown mare went lame

But most will agree
>	with the oldest barn wag
That if you love hunting,
>	then never hunt drag!

RACE DAY

Dawn breaks early misty light
As lingering fog escapes the night
While dew lies heavy on the ground
Where foxes lurk and prey abound.

Though silent now for its the day
When horses race and children play
While punters stand and study form
And try to quantify the norm.

As swiftly through the dampened grass
The grooms come leading horses past
With nostrils flaring blowing wide
Short stepping pace or lengthening stride.

While trainers stand with watchful eye
Or throw the jockeys stirrup high
To crouch above the horses back
Then springing trot down to the track.

Awhile to wait the starter's whim
And study other faces grim
The flag drops down, the cry, "they're off!"
The ladies sigh, the gentry scoff.

As equines leap into the hands
And cheers come from the hillside stands
The thundering hooves kick up the clods
And scar the lush green velvet sods.

Down to the hard packed fence of brush
The wide-eyed frenzied horses rush
Up and over the timbered pile
They lift and tuck in varied style.

Some will fall and splay the ground
While others make a cleaner bound
To gallop on and hug the rail
With head outstretched and flying tail.

Around the curve and up the hill
Where other hurdles claim a spill
The back stretch looms, the way looks clear
But now a loose horse may appear.

Ride carefully now, what he may do
Could spell disaster for a few
By now the field is opening out
As watchers start to scream and shout.

The last big fence stands wide and green
The leaders take it high and clean
Although a challenger could fall
A rider thought he knew it all!

The final turn demands decision
As riders jostle for position
To move inside before the straight
Or stay up close to sit and wait.

It's all a game the jockeys play
In hopes the move will "make their day"
The third horse makes a sudden spurt
A sour-faced shyster sheds his shirt.

The finish line approaches fast
As riders save their best for last
With whip in hand the leaders flail
The trainers groan, the owners pale.

But win or lose they all agree
No matter what your sport may be
There's nothing that can meet the pace
Nor match the thrill of Steeplechase.

CROSS-COUNTRY

The cross-country phase in eventing,
    requires a high degree of skill
And a careful amount of planning,
    to obtain the adrenalin thrill.

Faith in your horse is essential,
    with a mutual feeling of trust
Fitness and strength potential,
    and knowing the course is a must.

You must know where you are going,
    it matters not where you have been
Rhythm and pace must keep flowing,
    if you are to cross the line clean.

Fences will frequently vary,
    in structure position and height
A few will appear quite scary,
    particularly on bends that are tight.

Designers are devious fellows,
    who endeavor to give of their best!
By using steep slopes and deep hollows,
    to give you the ultimate test.

Jumps are meant to look natural,
    as nature designed them to be
But often the man-made obstacle,
    is not crossed so easily.

Courses were never selected,
    by farmers or landed gentry
Barriers and walls were erected,
    to stop wild animal entry.

A long-sided trough serves the herd,
    while a steep coop provides chicken feed
Tall hedges and brush test the nerd.
    and a log bench demands special heed.

Some fences appear convoluted,
    builders have carte blanche it is known
All types of designs are thought suited,
    that landsmen would never have shown.

Take the Y trap or X box or Zigzag,
    or rubber tires rolled into line
They were never conceived by a farm wag,
    however mischievous his time.

A flat level feeder for pheasants,
    a huge table and chairs for a giant
A vegetable stand for the peasants,
    a triple rail drop dares each client.

The elephant trap scares the horses,
    the narrow wood style is a test
Designed say reliable sources,
    to stop you from giving your best.

Sheep pens, wide ditches and banks,
    water that checks your true flight
Constructed by crazies and cranks,
    to test your courage and might.

Such is the thrill of eventing,
    you'll try it again and again
Without ever a thought of dissenting,
    in spite of the physical strain.

Whatever the risk it is worth it
    For both rider and equine friend
Forget the bright ribbon you forfeit
    Make sure you're both there at the end.!

COMBINED DRIVING
PRESENTATION

When riders reach a certain age
They move to another stage
Instead of sitting astride a horse
They pursue a different course.

Competitive Driving is a sport
That satisfies the thrill they've sought
Three-Day-Event rules are applied
To Combined Driving now worldwide.

So let's consider current rules
Then we will never look like fools
Dressage, Marathon and Obstacle phases
Are three of four required stages.

But before the dressage test can be
There's Presentation Stationary
Turnout must be of the highest state
Make sure your team is looking great.

Drivers are judged on their standard of dress
While grooms are not judged any the less
Harness and tack are closely inspected
To ensure that safety has not been neglected.

All that's on show must practically gleam
Carriage and gear should be scrupulously clean
Horses must be in excellent condition
If you are to avoid a drop in position.

Once you've completed inspection at large
You can move on to the dreaded Dressage!

DRESSAGE

There are singles, pairs or more in hand
All may be entered if that's what is planned.

Every movement must be so exact.
Driver and team must never detract
From any movement that is written down
If you miss out on one the judge will frown.

There's the walk and trot, the figure of eight
Make sure transitions do not come through late.
Tight bend and circles, the awkward rein back
All of the hooves should fall straight on the track.

Dressage means training of the exceptional kind
While you are competing bear that in mind.
It will never be easy you may not get it right
But keep persevering then one day you might.

Halt square at X give the judge a salute
Then prepare for the exciting Marathon Route!

THE MARATHON PHASE

The Marathon phase is a test of endurance
With a well-trained team you will have some assurance
But if either your horse or team are unfit
You will have cause to worry a bit.

The order of start is always provided
By previous scores that are already decided
Walk, trot and canter are again decreed
You can try a brief gallop but really no need.

Resist the temptation to move out and race
Better to stay at a more regular pace
Courses are twisty and tiring in length
Which demands a quick eye and obvious strength.

Hazards can cause a great deal of concern
With back-ups and water and difficult turns
Just keep on moving and hold them in hand
Then you'll finally end up where you planned.

Horses must take compulsory rests
To ensure they always perform at their best
And it's very exciting for spectators too
Who admire good driving, it's all up to you!

OBSTACLES

The obstacle course requires great concentration
Before you or your team can obtain satisfaction
Hazards are placed in the original area
Where dressage was held but now a bit scarier.

Rules are similar to Stadium Jumping
But instead of a pole the cone takes the thumping
If the ball is displaced from the top of the cone
The driver will surely have reason to groan.

Approaches are made from different directions
If you miss any one, expect some corrections
Penalty points are awarded for sure
Which definitely adds to the negative score.

Take extra care when crossing the water
The horse will decide if he really ought-a!
Let your prior training give obvious witness
That this is a test of your horse's true fitness.

It may be a fact that you no longer ride
But at least you will still have a horse on your side!

TODAY

Today I walked through meadows green
Paused beside a rushing stream
To watch a white cloud floating by
Reflected from the distant sky

Along a leafy path I strolled
Past stile and logs all sideways rolled
Up to the bridge of rough grey stone
Where I had never been alone.

Down the hill and through the lane
I followed tracks that once were plain
But now those marks I knew so well
Were crossed by ones I could not tell.

Then I found a rusty shoe
Amongst the leaves all wet with dew
And memories came rushing back
Of early mornings on a hack.

When we would go together there
In weather foul and weather fair
And feel the wind upon our faces
Carrying the scent of unknown places.

Of fox and rabbit, dog and hare
While naked branches bent to tear
To separate us from each other
While we went on to re-discover.

Unusual birds and beasts and flowers
Such happy carefree glorious hours
But now alas we go no more
Where we had often gone before.

Quite unashamed I stood and cried
For today my friend, my horse, he died.

(In memory of "Wilton")

I SAW A HORSE

I saw a horse today, a big beautiful bay

He came across the field at a trot
And stood by the gate where the car had stopped.
He stared at us with his big brown eyes
And swished his tail at the troublesome flies.

He stomped and scraped the grassy ground
Sending the tufts flying around
Then he snorted and blew as we moved near
Though he didn't show the slightest fear.

As I stroked him all over and picked up his feet
So I gave him a carrot as a little treat
Then he galloped around showing off for a while
One couldn't help but admire his style.

I pulled on his halter and led him inside
He stood up so tall and filed out with pride
Then accepted the saddle and bridle so good
I mounted with care from a low stump of wood.

He trotted on up to the sandy ring
And didn't object to a single thing
Whatever I asked he accomplished with ease
As if he was really trying to please.

Then we moved out to the country beyond
Down the long lane that skirted the pond
We walked past the poplars that reached for the sly
And splashed through the creek that went hurrying by.

With hardly a stumble or break in his stride
O'er ditches and banks freely and wide
With mane and tail flying we rode with the wind!
Somehow I knew I had found a new friend.

So I bought a horse today, a big beautiful bay!

IN YOUR HANDS

In your hands lies the power
Of the most intelligent, patient,
Willing, courageous, powerful
Yet most frustrating dumb animal on earth.

Earn his trust, his obedience,
His gratitude and his friendship
Then and only then, can you say
You are a "Horseman!"
       John Anthony Davies

ABOUT THE AUTHOR

John Anthony Davies was born near London, England from Welsh Ancestry. Thirteen years of military service included tours of duty in the Far East, Middle East, and Western Europe. During the last three years, he was Head Instructor at a Military Saddle Club.

In 1959, John trained and rode with the Military Club's Team and the International Horse Show, White City Stadium, London. The same year, he qualified for the British Horse Society's Instructor's Certificate.

From 1960 – 1963, Davies held the post of Director/Trainer at the South London School of Equitation, teaching therapeutic horsemanship.

In 1964, he accepted the position of Director/Chief Instructor at the Chigwell Trust Center, the first purpose-built establishment in the world designed solely for the rehabilitation of disabled children and adults through equestrian therapy. The Trust was one of the founding members of the British Association.

In 1966, he wrote "The Reins of Life," the first manual ever published describing his teaching methods, now adopted internationally. Published by J.A. Allen & Co. London. Reprinted with a foreword by H.R.H. Princess Anne. The poem "I Saw a Child" in the book is known internationally. Three additional books are published.

Acknowledged as one of the foremost authorities on therapeutic horsemanship, he became an adviser to the French, German, Dutch, Canadian, and American National

Associations, also consultant to the first purpose-built facility in America, the Cheff Therapeutic Riding Center in Battle Creek, Michigan.

In 1972, elected President of the North American Association (NARHA) for three consecutive terms. Now known as the Professional Association for Therapeutic Horsemanship (PATH) it is the national advisory body in America.

He was an examiner for the National Instructor Certification Program and a member of the Center Accreditation Committee. As Past President, liaised between the United States and Canada and represented NARHA at International Conferences on Therapeutic Riding. In 1996, he became a naturalized citizen of the United States and now lives in retirement in Florida.

www.XenophonPress.com

Xenophon Press is dedicated to the preservation of classical equestrian literature. We bring both new and old works to English-speaking riders.

30 Years with Master Nuno Oliveira, Henriquet 2011

A Journey Through the Horse's Body, Fritz 2012

A Rider's Survival from Tyranny, de Kunffy 2012

Another Horsemanship, Racinet 1994

Austrian Art of Riding, Poscharnigg 2015

Broken or Beautiful: The Struggle of Modern Dressage, Barbier/Conrod 2020

Classic Show Jumping: the de Nemethy Method, de Nemethy 2016

Classical Dressage with Anja Beran, Beran 2017

Divide and Conquer Book 1, Lemaire de Ruffieu 2016

Divide and Conquer Book 2, Lemaire de Ruffieu 2017

Dressage for the 21st Century, Belasik 2001

Dressage in the French Tradition, Diogo de Bragança 2011

Dressage Principles and Techniques: A Blueprint for the Serious Rider, Tavora 2018

Dressage Principles Illuminated, Expanded Edition, de Kunffy 2021

Dressage Sabbatical: A Year of Riding with Classical Master Paul Belasik, Caslar 2016

École de Cavalerie Part II, Robichon de la Guérinière 2015

Elements of Dressage, von Ziegner 2016

Equestrian Art Collected Works, Nuno Oliveira 2021

Equine Osteopathy: What the Horses Have Told Me, Giniaux 2014

Equitation, Bussigny 2021

Fragments from the Writings of Max Ritter von Weyrother, Fane 2017

François Baucher: The Man and His Method, Baucher/Nelson 2013
General Chamberlin: America's Equestrian Genius, Matha 2020
Great Horsewomen of the 19th Century in the Circus, Nelson 2015
Gymnastic Exercises for Horses Volume II, Eleanor Russell 2013
H. Dv.12 German Cavalry Manual of Horsemanship, Reinhold 2014
Handbook of Jumping Essentials, Lemaire de Ruffieu 2015
Handbook of Riding Essentials, Lemaire de Ruffieu 2015
Healing Hands, Giniaux, DVM 1998
Horse Training: Outdoors and High School, Beudant 2014
I, Siglavy, Asay 2018
Horsemanship & Horsemastership Volume 1, US Cavalry 2021
Horsemanship Training Films 3 DVD set, US Cavalry 2021
Learning to Ride, Santini 2016
Legacy of Master Nuno Oliveira, Millham 2013
Lessons in Lightness: Expanded Edition, Mark Russell 2019
Methodical Dressage of the Riding Horse, Faverot de Kerbrech 2010
Military Equitation or, A Method of Breaking Horses, and Teaching Soldiers to Ride, Pembroke, and *A Treatise on Military Equitation*, Tyndale 2018
My Horses Have Something to Say, de Wispelaere 2021
Principles of Dressage and Equitation, a.k.a. Breaking and Riding, Fillis 2017
Racinet Explains Baucher, Racinet 1997
Releasing the Jaw, Poll, and Neck DVD, Mark Russell 2021
Riding and Schooling Horses, Chamberlin 2020
Riding by Torchlight, Cord 2019
Riding in Rhyme, Davies 2021
Schooling Exercises In Hand, Hilberger 2009
Science and Art of Riding in Lightness, Stodulka 2015
Sketches of the Equestrian Art, Barbier/Sauvat 2021
The Art of Riding a Horse, D'Eisenberg 2015
The Art of Traditional Dressage, Volume 1 DVD, de Kunffy 2013
The Chamberlin Reader, Chamberlin/Matha, 2020

The de Nemethy Method: A training seminar, 8 DVD set, de Nemethy 2019
The Ethics and Passions of Dressage Expanded Edition, de Kunffy 2013
The Forward Impulse, Santini 2016
The Gymnasium of the Horse, Steinbrecht 2018
The Horses, a novel, Walker 2015
The Italian Tradition of Equestrian Art, Tomassini 2014
The Maneige Royal, de Pluvinel 2010, 2015
The New Method of Dressing Horses a.k.a. A General System of Horsemanship, Cavendish 2020
The Portuguese School of Equestrian Art, de Oliveira/da Costa 2012
The Quest for Lightness in Equitation and Equestrian Questions, Nelson/L'Hotte 2021
The Spanish Riding School & Piaffe and Passage, Decarpentry 2013
The Spanish Riding School: The Miracle of the White Horse DVD, US Lipizzan Association 2021
To Amaze the People with Pleasure and Delight, Walker 2015
Total Horsemanship, Racinet 1999
Training Hunters, Jumpers, and Hacks, Chamberlin 2019
Training Your Foal, Ettl 2011
Training with Master Nuno Oliveira, 2 DVD set, Eleanor Russell 2016
Truth in the Teaching of Master Nuno Oliveira, Eleanor Russell 2015
Wisdom of Master Nuno Oliveira, de Coux 2012

www.ingramcontent.com/pod-product-compliance
Lightning Source LLC
Chambersburg PA
CBHW060532010526
44110CB00052B/2572